The Miracle Wheel
Hearing God for a Game Show

Published through Create Space 2016
ISBN-13:978-1503346789
ISBN-10:1503346781

Cover Painting ~ Karah Winkler
Interior formatting and design ~ Vince Corcoran
Final Editing Help – Katie Knepler

Scripture quotations used;

New International Version
New Living Translation
New Century Translation
English Standard Version
New American Standard Version

*For more information, to order books or schedule a
speaking engagements please visits website:
cristislife.com*

*To order online in print and also in Kindle:
http://www.amazon.com/dp/B01B6K52FU?ref_=pe_2427
780_160035660*

The Miracle Wheel

Hearing God for a Game Show

By Cristi Winkler

To Mom

Thank you so much for your powerful prayers and your constant encouragement to me in my life. You were the most beautiful gift that God could ever give to anyone and I will forever be grateful.

Acknowledgements

Thank you first and foremost to the Lord Jesus, God, my wonderful father, and savior and best friend. I also want to thank my mother, not only for her love and prayers but also for encouraging me to audition for Wheel of Fortune. Thank you to my awesome sons, Paul and Mat for their support and love. I also want to thank my spiritual mentors/mothers Joyce Moyer, Jayne Steiner and Julie Joyner. Your precious time, compassionate ears and words of wisdom have forever changed me. I also want to thank all of the people who have helped me with the editing and structuring of this book. There are too many to mention but among them are Karah Winkler for your amazing painting for this book and your time in editing. Jessica Kaehne, Carol Albert and Judith Morrison for your wonderful editing help and encouragement, Cynthia Bell for your creative talents for my book design, Rick Joyner for wisdom and nudges for me to get this book done.

Also... a very special thank you to Katie Knepler, you are one the biggest blessings God could ever send in someone's life. I couldn't have done this without you. You asked me a few years ago to be your spiritual mother but yet you have blessed my life more than I could have ever imagined. You make me better than I am. Thank you for staying committed with me by your selfless giving of your time for this book, I am forever grateful for you in my life.

Note to Reader

As you journey through the pages of this book, you will come to hear a powerful testimony that only God could have thought up. There are many years in the making of this book to share what God put together—and many attempts from the enemy of God to stop this book from becoming a reality. There were many financial losses, emotional attacks, and supernatural disappearances of files of this book, not just with me but also for many people who have attempted to help with it. So, if you are reading this book it is because of God's angel armies that fought in the spiritual realm for it's existence.

Also note that miracles have taken place in peoples lives after hearing this amazing testimony. I believe that you too can also be a recipient of God's divine blessings that come from the power of a testimony.

Revelation 12:11

"And they overcame him because of the blood of the Lamb and because of the word of their testimony, and they did not love their life even when faced with death."

James 1:2-3

"Dear brothers and sisters, when troubles of any kind come your way, consider it an opportunity for great joy. For you know that when your faith is tested, your endurance has a chance to grow."

Table Of Contents

Chapter One

God's Character

One of my most treasured masterpieces is hanging in my kitchen. It is a picture of a black spotted cow surrounded by a beautiful green pasture and a vivid red barn with a small yellow door handle. My youngest son painted this magnificent showpiece when he was 7 years old. I am proud to say that I am the sole owner of it. It is famous to anyone who has eaten in any of my kitchens. It captures the heart. At least it does mine. Leonardo Da Vinci, eat your heart out.

Like us, God is very excited about the new things He created. We too can become quite enthusiastic to show off our creations of art but and even more so our children. Imagine God telling everyone to look at how beautiful the daffodils turned out. "Look how loudly they put forth their trumpets for all the world to see". There is a poem about daffodils written by the poet William Wordsworth in 1888 titled "I Wandered Lonely as A Cloud." William explains how the daffodils dance—and even danced better than the waves. He also shares in this poem that these daffodils give him joy. This joy has replaced his loneliness. Every time he is sad or lonely he thinks about these daffodils as if he were dancing with them.

On the last day of God's creation, He decided to make mankind (Genesis 1:27). He made man in His own image—male and female. There are many days when I would look at my body and wonder, "What was He thinking?!" I may never know, but He is the Creator and I need to be grateful for the opportunity of being created. God tells us that He created us in His image (Genesis 1:27). If we were created in God's image, then we were created to be creative as God is creative. God also tells us in scripture about His other characteristics such as our comforter, our provider, our Prince of Peace, etc. God is merciful, compassionate, kind and caring. He is wise and all knowing, powerful and unchanging. God compares Himself to a lion as well as an eagle and even a lamb. We can find so much more about Him as we seek Him out in His Word and in our relationship with Him.

We may at times be angry at Him because we don't understand why bad things are happening in our lives but we can trust that it is not something He created us for. Instead we are living out the consequences from the spiritual fall in the Garden of Eden. Satan since then has had dominion in the world, but God tells us that in a short while we will have no more pain, suffering, sorrow or anything that would cause us to be anxious and afraid. He knows what the future holds, and Satan is defeated. There will be a new world order and we cannot even think or imagine the good things that God has for us if we choose to be His. We can trust that His character is who He says He is. He will always turn the bad for His good purposes (Romans 8:28).

When I was a teenager, I used to sneak a peek in the Bible on occasion. I also as a child experienced some teaching about Jesus in Bible studies that my mother would take me to with my younger siblings. I remember how I wanted this love to be true. I wished I could see this Jesus and ask Him to help my mother from my angry father. I wanted to know that this Jesus would stop the terrible things that my father would do and say to my mother, my family and myself. I wanted this Jesus to tell me it was okay for how I hated my father and to help me to understand that He loved me anyway. If I were to ask Him for anything for myself it would be that I would truly know that I was worth something and created for a reason.

I eventually lost interest in God, because He wasn't there to show Himself to me and other things began to preoccupy my time. It bothered me when our family would go to church only on holidays and that this church never seemed to tell me about that same Jesus that loved me. The only message I got from the long and boring sermons were that if I wasn't going to that particular church every week that I would be doomed for hell. They did seem to offer religious alternative duties to earn my way back to going to heaven but we never pursued that. I couldn't understand why my parents would even go at all if we were already facing eternal damnation. In searching for Jesus, as I occasionally was, I unfortunately never found Him there. I also never seemed to find him in my Bible searching either. All I ever seemed to find was an angry and arrogant God that I would never be good enough for. He seemed bent on revenge with His enemies. I must have always opened it to the wrong places and assumed that it was telling me what God was about. I since then have come to understand that most of the violence in the old testament is a representation or foreshadow to our spiritual fight against the true demonic enemies of God in the spiritual realm. We no longer fight flesh and blood but instead against powers and principalities of darkness and evil in the heavenly realm. We do this with prayer and intercession here on earth. See Ephesians 6:12. Our authority over the demonic spirits is through the name of Jesus and His spirit in us.

This God in the bible that I would read about was also was known as the *Father* in heaven. Go figure.

I occasionally came across televangelists shouting that I was a sinner and needed to repent. I already knew I wasn't good enough. They didn't have to rub it in more. I gave up my search even though I still felt something like His presence inside me at times. He was like a lost lover never to be found. I then started to fill that feeling with other things like alcohol, drugs, food—I even inhaled spray deodorant when I was 12 years old. I wanted to stop what was going on inside of me, but those other things never seemed to satisfy what was missing. I hated the smell of alcohol because of my father. I swore to myself when I was young that I would never drink.

There are times when God says He is angry in the Bible and even uses the word "hate." That is not God's character the way we think it is. God's character is love. God's hate is known as a "perfect hate". It is a hate that is for anything that is not of Him because He is love. His love is pure. He created us with a conscience to be able to distinguish what is immoral from what is good. Some people call a longing for Him a God-shaped hole that only He can fill. That must have been what was going on with me. I was living my life with a big God-shaped hole inside my heart.

My first experience with understanding God was the day His Holy Spirit nudged me off the floor and onto the phone with the treatment center. My God-shaped hole was now in overwhelming pain. While lying there inside my head, there was screaming going on, "I can't do this any longer. This is enough." I had hit my bottom, and it seemed I couldn't go any lower. The only real good I felt I had done in my life, that proved to be of any meaning, was being a mother to my children. I wanted a better life for my children and to give them a healthier mom. By the prompting of the Holy Spirit and years of wanting freedom from the bar life, I checked myself into treatment and it was the start of my new life. My husband at the time could never give me what I truly needed even though I am sure he wanted to. I hurt him by making the decision to start my new life without him. I repeatedly told him while we were married that I needed us to change our lives from the way were living, but we never did. We didn't seem to know how — even if we wanted to. We actually never even searched it out. He didn't feel the same convictions that I was having and I needed to find myself.

I declared Jesus as my "higher power" in Alcoholics Anonymous. I attended for 5 years after treatment and then began to consider converting to Judaism. An orthodox Jewish friend in AA led me to a nice job where I started to learn the Torah and became responsible to keep things "kosher", especially in the kitchen. I often would cry on my way home from working there, because I wanted to be doing things for God like they were doing. These Jewish people celebrated God more days than we worked it seemed. The Lord then redirected me. I would have never found Jesus in Judaism. My friend, Jayne Steiner, kept inviting me to her church, and I finally realized that it was something I should try. After all Jesus was my higher power, and I was already reading some Christian material with my devotions. I loved this church from the start. The worship music ministered to my soul. Up until then, I never really knew that churches would play rock music for God but only knew of the old hymns. The Pastor's messages about God were in line with the steps that I knew in AA. The church was Victory Christian Fellowship and the Pastor was Ted Moyer. I was very excited to be even closer in my search for the Jesus that loved me. This pastor then led me to understand that I didn't need God and AA but that all I needed was God alone. He helped me to understand that I was not an alcoholic, but, in Jesus, I am an overcomer. Jayne started putting books into my hands to read as well as music. She prayed with me and baptized me. One of the books Jayne gave me that made a huge impact on my life is written by Rick Joyner, The Final Quest. This book gave me a glimpse of a whole new chapter of hope in my life and a deeper understanding of the spiritual battle that living as a Christian we face. I wanted to have this deeper understanding of God and was amazed at what God was giving Rick to write in this book. I found a new understanding of myself as part of the army of God that brought me into a new way to worship Jesus and understand Him. I replaced my AA Big Book with the Bible. I, in my obsession while reading the scriptures, would find myself sometimes in a struggle with God for answers to what seemed contradictory to me. I didn't trust to hear the opinions on this to anyone else but God. I made a pact with God that He had to teach me what truth that He wanted me to know and believe in. He never seemed to mind. He started to often answer me at stoplights and I would realize it was Him. He is not an angry God but instead became my friend.

Victory eventually had a church split. I was devastated, but now instead of a church to focus on I was able to go deeper alone with God. I have had different experiences in the church. Some good and some bad since then, but have come to realize that what was told to me that first day I checked myself into treatment happened to be the best advice to start my new journey. I was told, "Take what you need and leave the rest." I eventually began to attend other churches and became a part of different ministries and found that the Lord desires us to seek Him and His word in order to find where He is leading us next. He has plans and purposes for us, to give us a hope and a future (Jeremiah 29:11) but it may not be the way we think it should be. I don't believe God ever wants churches to split but He will take what is bad and always turn it for His good purposes.

One night while reading in the bible the story about Balaam, I was amazed at how Balaam ignored the warnings of God so much that he even disregarded the weirdness of his own donkey talking to him. He kept doing things his own way. This I have come to know through a quote as, "self will run riot". Balaam's mind was set on a plan to make things happen successfully in his own way (Genesis 22). So often we have zeal to do what is right for God's kingdom, but if God is not in it we will not be making the difference that we originally hoped to make. I noticed that some preachers can also put yokes on their congregations to contend for their blessing so God will make big things happen for them in their lives. I don't think these pastors mean to put this burden of needing something to be better, but may not realize that may be taking away from the gratitude of the small yet powerful things God is doing in their lives today. It is wonderful to give hope but not if it conveys an underlying message of seeking for self. This yoke of blessing can create what God never meant to be on us. I also believe that it can convey a message that some day we will be "somebody special" for the kingdom of God when in reality we already are. We are and will always be important and special to God. Jesus seemed to stress that the kingdom of heaven is different from the world. When things look weak to the world we seem to assume that God is not blessing it. Imagine being one of the disciples when the Messiah is beaten and hung on a cross. It doesn't look too good, yet it was one of the most powerful things that took place for God's kingdom. The disciples seemed to repeatedly want revenge on whoever was against Jesus, all for good reasons, but Jesus always seemed to convey the message that the kingdom of God is not about getting back or taking revenge or even having dominion in areas, but coming to know love and helping others to find this love. This in itself is being a part of the power of the kingdom of heaven. Mother Theresa held dying babies lying in gutters so these babies were not alone when they died. We were given authority over demons with Jesus' name but we need to question what are we being authoritative over and is it the way God's kingdom works. If God is calling someone to take back the land, then that is what they should do as long as they are doing it in love, but I truly believe that some may be missing out on the humble character of God by being so caught up in the fight for God's kingdom and blessings. It actually can easily bring our countenance to one of arrogance rather than humility.

God gives and takes away. Some people are blessed with prosperity and some even to help the world politically, but if we are after power for the kingdom of God, without God, we are not really helping His kingdom at all. The disciples even got caught up in competition wanting to be better than the other. God knows the intensions of our hearts even though, at times, we become so blind to what we are doing. Without love, we are just a noisy cymbal, (1 Corinthians 13:1). God desires us to know that He is about love. If we trust Him and His character we can have peace that He knows what is going on and knows everything even from the beginning to the end. In a world of chaos, it is hard for us not to be anxious, but the more we do, the better we become at it—like with any exercise or sport. God may not be calling us for something big as the world see's as big, but we can trust that He is calling us to love. There is that old saying, "bloom where we are planted" and even though we may not feel we are being significant, God's character will bear fruit in our lives as we allow Him. God has always led me in things that I never planned myself, and I would then just have to adjust and learn and grow in the new surroundings.

I had a friend in AA named Mike. He, like me, was

transitioning from AA to join the church. He lived in a different town and a different congregation but often we would drive half way to get together and share the spiritual things that God was doing and teaching us in our lives. My brother, Marty, was dying in the hospital and Mike and I decided to go and share the message of God to Marty in hopes that he would hear us through his unconsciousness. I laid my hands on Marty and started to pray for him. The medical machines that Marty was hooked up to started to make loud noises with lights flashing everywhere. I was taken back in surprise. It seemed like every doctor and nurse that worked in the hospital came running into the room and told us to leave while they took care of the chaos. I was never told by the hospital what happened, but I knew that something was happening in the spiritual realm. Mike mentioned that it was not from God. God doesn't do the same things he did years ago in the Bible. I dared him to read his bible again. It seems unnatural to me to give only power to Satan, and for God's to be outdated and useless. God's heart is for us to bring the Kingdom of Heaven to Earth (Matthew 6:10). God gives us authority here on Earth by Jesus' Holy Spirit (that came after His death and resurrection). Jesus is alive by His Spirit and resides in us (Galatians 2:20), and our power comes from Him. We were not only created in the likeness of God, but now have Him living inside us. My brother, Marty, passed away, and it could easily be thought that God's power was not there, but I believe that Marty heard us and gave His life to Jesus and there was a battle in the spiritual realm for his soul. I will see him again one day. I am sure of it.

If we are created in His image, as emotional beings, God must be an emotional God as I mentioned earlier with some of His characteristics. Many places in scripture God also refers to Himself as a jealous God. His jealousy cannot be compared to the world's jealousy though. His is out of pure love. Ours is usually because of some competitive or prideful spirit wanting us to be the one who benefits. His love is true and for our benefit. He desires that we will not love anything more than Him, because He is the one that holds our future. He is the comforter and the healer. He is the one who can keep us safe. If our lives are lived at a distance from Him, we cannot truly experience His love and presence in our lives. Imagine a wife longing for her husband's love but his mind is still on figures for a proposal for his business. He is at work in his mind while spending time with his wife. The wife is not the center of her husband's love and devotion and he is in a position to lose her, as she desires to be intimately loved and for him to be devoted to her alone. We, too, can lose sight of God's love and presence, because we get so caught up in other things. Even in church, we can be far from actually thinking of Him, worshipping Him, or spending time with Him, yet He longs for our love and devotion to Him alone.

Too often we get caught up in feeling the need to earn his love and acceptance the way we might of our own earthly father. Religious laws can create this kind of thinking. There are man made laws that God never intended for us. The laws that are in the Old Testament no human could ever fulfill and have been completely fulfilled by Jesus' blood.

Imagine a family with a pet dog that repeatedly has accidents on the floor. This dog means the world to its family and nothing it could do would separate the family's feelings for it. They might be disappointed but always ready to snuggle again with open arms. There are many that have shared of my former thoughts of God as being an owner ready to punish if we make messes of our lives. However, those thoughts are not of God and not what God is about. Elizabeth in Pride and Prejudice thought of Mr. Darcy as a cold and arrogant man. She scoffed at the thought of him wanting a relationship with her, but once she spent time with him and got to know the true motives of his heart and how they were in the best interest for others, she fell in love with him. She received the idea that this man could love her as well. She wanted to be around him whenever she could, she wanted to talk to him, she was up all hours of the night thinking about him. Her whole world revolved around him. Imagine God, emotionally giddy and dancing and spinning because of His love for you.

Someday there will be no more pain or sorrow—no guilt or fear. In the movie "Inside Out", we can come to understand that Sadness is an important part of our emotional balance, especially for our conscience. In scripture there is a world that someday will not need sadness, because in the atmosphere of the Lord, there is peace and joy and we will be complete and whole in Him.

I also want to share before moving on that in this testimony regarding the wheel is that God is a God of kindness. His kindness has changed me more than anything else. I found His love so amazing in His kindness. It is so powerful that it changes a heart. I love the story about the poor man in Victor Hugo's book and movie "Les Miserables". The ex-convict Jean Valjean stole from a rich man who had given him food and lodging. Instead of being arrested, he was instead shown mercy and kindness. This rich man reversed Jean's fate by presenting a scenario to the police that he gave Jean these items and even presented more expensive items that were supposedly left behind. This rich man never really gave Jean any of these things but yet was giving this appearance to the police that he had while also still giving the things to Jean. This act of compassion had not only given Mr. Valjean a new perception of grace but it also very powerfully changed his heart and life. In that moment, Jean no longer wanted to steal or live the way he had always lived before, but instead began to live a life with a changed character. He went from stealing to giving, even to the point of caring for an orphan girl that needed a father. Jean became repentant, humbled and changed and in by being blessed he also had become a blessing.

As we find God's character of love and grace, we too are changed. We are an important creation to God.

We, like the daffodils, are beautiful in God's sight. He longs to have a love relationship with us. Any time He thinks of us, it brings Him joy.

Zephaniah 3:17

"The Lord your God is with you, The Mighty Warrior who saves. He will take great delight in you; In His love He will no longer rebuke you, but will rejoice over you with singing."

Psalm 86:15

"But you, Lord, are a compassionate and gracious God, slow to anger, abounding in love and faithfulness."

Chapter Two

God's Manifest Presence

There are so many different ideas about God as well as life, nature, and love. Some people only see God in theology and miss out on knowing Him personally. I want to mention that the story I am telling in this book has everything to do with God. It is God's real life intervention. It is something I want to share with the world, and my desire is for everyone to know the Lord in this personal way. I have had the opportunity to see His manifest presence even before being saved. He was nudging me and doing things inside of me that were very real. So far, he has shown himself in other supernatural ways. The living God wants to show His presence in our lives.

My first experience was at home in my bathroom. I was working on Step 6 in AA, where "we become ready to have God remove all of our defects of character." I wondered and asked my sponsor, who was guiding me through the steps, when I could move on. In my (humble I thought) opinion, I was learning so much and doing so well that I must be ready to take on what was next which was Step 7 "asking God to remove our shortcomings." I previously had written a thorough inventory of my whole life and had the opportunity to see before me in paper all of my past relationships. This was not easy. It involved all who had hurt me, who I was angry with, and then the last column came with what my reactions were to each person's faults and wrongdoings. I learned so many things about myself I had not realized before this or never really even thought about. As far as I was concerned, I was a victim and thought it only fair to justify my own actions to what I experienced. What was now taking place was that the blinders were being removed and I had to see myself for who I really was for the first time. It was kind of like choking on a grape.

Too often we go through life with blinders on. It seems one of my "character defects," which in AA is a nice way of saying "sin", is to become defensive or bitter and hold grudges without expressing myself in a healthy way. I still cannot say I am the greatest at it, but God is working on that in me. In James 1:24 we find a very important truth about ourselves. It states that we look in the mirror and walk away forgetting what we look like. I think too often we just don't want to deal with hard realities about ourselves because we don't know how to change and don't take the time to do something about our weaknesses. We just ignore them and try to become comfortable with who we are but then wonder why we cannot sleep at night.

I didn't understand why my sponsor was holding me back from moving on. I thought I was more than ready until one particular evening. I was applying make up in front of my bathroom mirror, and tears started to flow moving the make up down my chin as I wept. I felt God's presence more than ever in my life. I had done so many devotional readings and praying but now at this moment, He had a grip on my heart and I couldn't stand. I laid on the floor and wept some more. The thought of looking at myself in the mirror was unbearable. I seemed to have been on the Lord's operating table, and He was the surgeon that was going deep inside me digging up what was not good in me—and it hurt. In a groaning voice, I asked God to please remove every shortcoming in me that would cause me to hurt others. I had now completed Step 7, even though the steps didn't really matter any longer. It was ok with me if I stayed there on the floor in God's presence forever and never took another step. God's timing for things in our lives is so different from the way we would think they should be. I have also learned an ironic lesson in humility: once you claim you are humble and you've got it, it's gone.

What I have been learning of Jesus and His life is that He was humble but not a push over. He stood by what He was teaching and was not swayed by what others thought of Him. He had a purpose. Today in our culture it seems that our purpose is to be someone. To be popular is to be successful and important. The kingdom of God is different. The Bible says that even the smallest things we do for Him here are huge in heaven, especially if we are not getting the glory from it and God is. Many times our motives are to do great things for the kingdom but until God's surgery takes place we can become blind to our motives that involve the need to be somebody. I want to stress that if we are in a relationship with God we are already important. For example, big name conferences with evangelists and musicians can be used mightily for God in power and in healing people however God's favor isn't just in the popular. He is also in the small gatherings with any and everyone he chooses.

Jesus had a purpose and part of it entailed miracles. To name a few, He healed people (in weird ways I might add) like spitting on dirt and putting it on blind eyes or ears. He walked on water, changed water to wine, multiplied food, calmed storms, cursed a tree, caught a fish with a coin in it's mouth, raised a man from the dead, felt a woman touch his clothes in a crowd of people around Him. She touched His clothes wanting to be healed and He felt compassion. Nothing else mattered at that moment but for Him to find her and be Her God. Jesus' instructions are for us to finish what He started. In John 16:7 Jesus explains that He had to go so He could send the Holy Spirit, whom he refers to as "The Helper." That helper came in Acts chapter 2 in the form of what appeared as tongues of fire and a Holy drunkenness with bursts of laughter. Here again, might I add, that His ways are not our ways (Isaiah 55:8). There were many people in the room. This "Helper" was not just for the disciples of Jesus' time but very much are for us as well today. In Acts 2, when His Spirit came into that Upper Room there were 120 other people included not just Jesus' disciples. Charismatic experiences are often debated in the church, but if you have God's spirit inside of you, you are more apt to discern whether something is of God or if it is not. I often invite the Holy Spirit to show His presence in my life in a physical way—and He does.

One of my earliest experiences of the Acts 2 type of manifestations of God was at a church in Milwaukee. It started with a little old man, Joe Jordan, expressing excitedly how God use to show up once in a while but now He shows up EVERY TIME! People were laughing under the influence of the Holy Spirit. Joe invited the people of the church up to the stage for an alter call. While in the back of the line making my way up, I was contemplating the whole event. "Is this You God?" I was curious yet skeptical because I can be very untrusting at times. People were falling over on stage as they were being prayed for. I had seen this before and wasn't too

16

sure about it. If I had driven my car there I would have jumped in it and speed-tailed back home. I was stuck in line and decided to stick close to God with whatever was before me. I was with a friend I met from another church who had invited me with her sister. I had no clue what they were experiencing, but I was planning my escape. Once at the altar I would pretend to fall and hurry back to my seat. Surely I would feel safer in my seat. However God had something else planned. Somehow I never finished going through the line. I was supernaturally transported in time. One moment I was waiting in line, the next I was laying on my back at the altar. All over my body I felt heat that you would only feel if you were on fire. I was panicked and attempted to put out these flames. I then began to realize that the heat of this fire was not hurting me. I, was supernaturally touched, by God's "tongues of fire".

In reading the Old Testament, it talks about how God consumed the sacrifices with fire from heaven. It was like my life was a sacrifice on the altar and He touched me. After this amazing experience, I made my way down the stairs back to my safe seat. I clung to the railing because I felt tipsy. "What in the world! Am I drunk?" I thought. I hadn't had a drop of alcohol in 5 years but here I was drunker than ever before. I began to laugh. The laugh didn't stop but went on for the rest of the evening, even on our drive home. The two sisters in the front seats of the car were laughing so hard and no one was paying attention to the wheel. The Holy Spirit was driving the car as we headed down the highway home.

My cold, hard and untrusting heart that walked into that place, had left with an overflowing amount of joy. The next morning I had no hangover, no sore stomach and no remorse. What I had was an intense desire to look up every scripture verse that pertained to fire, being drunk, and laughing.

Isaiah 43:2
"When you walk through the fire, you will not be burned; the flames will not set you ablaze."

Deuteronomy 4:24
"For the LORD your God is a consuming fire; he is a jealous God." (See also Hebrews 12:29)

Acts 2:3
"They saw what seemed to be tongues of fire that separated and came to rest on each of them."

Ephesians 5:18
"And do not get drunk with wine, for that is debauchery, but be filled with the spirit."

Joel 2:28a
"In the last days, God says, I will pour out my Spirit on all people"

Job 8:21
"He will yet fill your mouth with laughter."

Other experiences of mine with God's presence includes a night when rushing winds came into my living room as I prayed with a young female. She was inquiring to hear about times I had experienced God's presence. I shared with her that God had given me open visions, I heard God's voice louder than thunder, I've had pennies that seemed to come from nowhere, I even found one in my pajama pockets. One woman that I prayed for in a ministries cafe in England saw a cloud appear above her hand. God was revealing His presence to her in a personal way through my praying for her. I saw a man be healed of cancer and many other miracles. I continued to share these experiences with the young woman and as we were talking and praying we experienced an amazing rush of wind come upon us. Her face appeared red as if the same tongues of fire were touching her that I experienced many years before. The living room blinds were clapping together and there were no windows or doors open to produce these breezes on us. God showed up. We felt His presence and it was wonderful. There was always a sense of God's presence that remained in that room thereafter.

The experience that impacted me the most was when my father was in the hospital and dying of cancer. My mother had moved away from him years before this. They sold the house and moved into separate apartments. She loved my father too much to divorce him but had finally made a way to find a new life for herself that would be safely away from my father when he would drink. Now, years later she was told that he would not be around much longer and to start making funeral arrangements. She thought it best to quickly move my father's things out of his apartment so it could be re-rented and she would be free of having to worry about his rent. She knew that my church, Victory Christian Fellowship, had been so closely knit in love and always there helping each other's needs that she asked me if they would come and take care of moving all of dad's things out. She didn't want any of it and offered everyone to take whatever they wanted and to give or throw the rest away. The church agreed and that Saturday got to work getting it done. Some of the guys seemed especially willing to find homes for his golf clubs.

Shortly after my mother was free of the apartment responsibility we were told that my father was getting worse and would not make it through the night week. Many of the family members took turns going in and spending time with him to say their goodbyes. I went and shared with him about Jesus. Because of the state he was in I wasn't sure if he heard me but I wanted to bring some kind of closure with my relationship with him there.

That next afternoon after grocery shopping I got home

and had a messages on my voicemail machine (for those of you who remember we had to wait to get home for our messages from a plugged in box!). This particular day my father was not supposed to make it through the night. As I listened to my messages there was an especially unusual message from a missionary minister, George from Africa who had been visiting our church that weekend. He informed me in this message that God spoke to him about my father "God is going to put a new song in your father's heart and a new dance in his feet". George said this with an urgency for me to call him before he departed out on his plane, which was soon. "Doesn't this guy understand that my father isn't suppose to make it through the night?" I thought to myself as I disregarded it and began to put my groceries away. Within the hour the phone rang and it was my mother. Her voice was quiet and somewhat concerned. "Chris" (note...only my family can call me Chris!), "the hospital just called and said that Dad is ok and they are releasing him from the hospital." I stopped what I was doing and couldn't believe what I was hearing. George's prophetic words from God about giving my father a new song and dance in his heart really could have been from God after all even though I had it in my mind that this could have meant in heaven and not here. How was my mother going to give the news to my father that everything he had was now gone?

My mother had him move into her spare room with the promise of no drinking. My father seemed to be doing good but I have to admit I didn't see the new song in his heart or dance in his feet because of the grumbling of his missing golf clubs! I also started petitioning God that night. "How could this man know so confidently that what he was hearing was really you Lord?" George's boldness of God's message to me about my father was given to me without a tinge of doubt that it was God. I also noticed that he had no worries about looking foolish if he had been wrong. "God I want to hear you like this" I cried. It was my cry to the Holy Spirit day and night. There seemed to be nothing else in this world that I wanted more.

I don't think God wants to be put in a religious box. He has many different ways of doing miracles in our lives and revealing His presence. This may look different for everyone, because everyone has a different relational experience with Jesus. His heart is to have a love relationship where we draw closer to hear Him. We can have faith that He will speak to us and reveal His presence—and that he is always there with us.

Deuteronomy 31:6

"...For the Lord your God goes with you; He will never leave you nor forsake you."

Jeremiah 33:3

"Call to me and I will answer you, and will tell you great and hidden things that you have not known"

Chapter Three

New Doors

In the Bible, the Israelites are a foreshadow of how God is in our lives today. Through historical events that they went through, it reveals that God was with them by leading them, guiding them, and feeding them. Even though it was hard because they were being led through a desert and had no home, God had a bigger plan. He was leading them out of a life of slavery to one of freedom and blessing.

I think of myself, at times, like an Israelite because of how my life has compared to their story. I was a single mom with two sons trying to make ends meet but found myself repeatedly losing jobs. I had to obtain new credit cards to supply my children with their needs in the interim of a new job. The companies I worked for were downsizing, or undergoing changes where I found myself in unfortunate job situations. The credit card debt started to increase and I began to question if God was still with me. While the Israelites were in the desert they often complained. This hurt the Lord because His heart was to help them. I made a pact with the Lord that I would not be like them and complain. My heart was to continuously trust Him and thank Him for the things that He had for me. Just as the Israelites, I, too, was in a place that I could not call home. I was in such debt, that I had to put my belongings in a storage unit. I took an offer from a very sweet woman, Theresa, who wanted to help me get back on my feet by offering me a room in her home. It was a bed to sleep in and a roof over my head, but I trusted that God was just having me pass through this desert.

When I moved in with Theresa, I questioned my self worth and where my life was going. Not only was I without my own home, but also was healing from the empty nest syndrome. My youngest son Mat had just moved to Pennsylvania after graduating from high school. He was grown now and had the right to make the choices he wanted to make for himself—even if I wasn't ready to give him up. I wasn't prepared for the pain I felt when he left. After years of being mom, both of my sons were off on their own and I needed to find a new role. I would no longer be able to cook or clean or share my life with my children the way I was able to when they were younger. It was a joy to fill our table with home cooked meals. Now I was preparing food for one. There was no more late night adventures to the video store and snuggling on our comfy couch with large bowls of popcorn. Throughout the years, I loved sharing the Lord with my children. We would take road trips to youth gatherings and conferences—now my home was void of even having them around to pray with.

Mat and I were invited to a conference at Morningstar Ministries in South Carolina just before he headed to out to his new life in Pennsylvania. Our close friends Randy and Jayne were driving out in their van and had extra room. We packed our bags and anticipated all that God would have for us there.

After the first day's events there was an opportunity for the attendees to be prayed over and receive prophetic words from God. Jayne and I were the first in line. We were led to a tent where the prophetic team had my name on the top of a list. The prophetic team prior to the conference, prayed about this list of names. The Holy Spirit revealed my name as one of several who God wanted to speak to. After the excitement of my name being on their list, this prophetic team began to pray for Jayne and me. They were all getting what seemed to be great revelations—very spiritual and encouraging. For me, one young man kept chiming in rather oddly about a wheel. I listened for my next big words of power and purpose that the Lord might have for me, but the young man then interrupted, and again brought up the wheel. He said, "wait I see the wheel with a horse and buggy--kind of an old fashioned type of wheel that used to be made out of wood." I nodded my head and thanked him and they proceeded to continue to give us our words. At the end, when it seemed that they were finished and before heading out of the tent, this young man with a sense of urgency looked at me and said "No, it's not a wheel with a horse and buggy, it is just a wheel and God is really going to use that wheel in your life!" I was amused at his excitement and thanked him for that word, but it didn't seem as urgent or important to me, because I didn't think much of it. I was impressed at his confidence of this message being from God to me. As we left the tent, I made a comment to Jayne sarcastically, "God is going to use a wheel in my life, okay...yeah right!" I thought it was the most absurd thing I had ever heard—or at least close to it. Even through my sarcasm I still wanted to be open to the fact that God may have plans to use a wheel in my life. God used a wheel in Ezekiel's life in the Bible, by giving him a very mysterious vision of a wheel that was within a wheel, why not mine?

That evening at the Morningstar conference, a man named John Chacha preached the meeting's message. He glowed with the most beautiful black skin. The room was hushed while listening to his Tanzanian accent give a message so profound that one couldn't help but believe God was speaking to them. "No more job... No more job, God is doing all new things. God is opening new windows, new doors, everything's new, nothing the same." I know the Lord was using John to speak this over me. "Noooooo!" The last thing I wanted was to go home and have no more job! I was trusting the Lord to keep me where I was, so I could get back on my feet. Yet, I could not deny what I felt in my spirit. That night when Randy, Jayne, Mat, and I met together after the meeting and snacking together, I kept being silly and repeating the message... "no more job" mockingly as if I were John Chacha. Randy looked at me quizzically and asked me what in the world I was talking about. I giggled and said, "I was being John Chacha." It turns out that what I heard about the job loss and new doors did not stand out to the others. We all went around and shared what stood out and each of us had gleaned something different from John's message that God was speaking to us personally. I seemed to know God was preparing me to lose my job again even though I didn't like it. He would be closing and opening new doors in my life.

When I was back at work, sure enough, the day came for my boss to give me the sad news: that he had to let me go because he was downsizing employees. I told him I already had prepared myself for this to happen because of John Chacha's message. As I was leaving, my boss handed me a wind up flashlight that he referred to as "a parting gift." I found it odd that he used a game show expression before sending me on my way. I said thanks and put my trust in the Lord as I walked out. I had a new flashlight that could light the way to my new door that God was opening. After all, I was one of His chosen people wandering in the desert and waiting for him to lead me out into my promised land.

In a new job search, I considered the word "wheel" to be a job at Wells Fargo. It revealed an old fashioned wheel with horses and a buggy. I thought, "This must be the wheel that will change my life!" It definitely would be a new door because I had no experience in banking, stocks, bonds or Wall Street. If I were to get hired there I would definitely be facing a new territory.

I shined up my resume, set up the interview, pulled from my closet my interview suit and prepared to look the part of Wall Street. I entered the interview with confidence that if the Lord was leading me there that I would be hired. The interview went well and my confidence in the Lord then carried me to a second interview. The man in the second interview however, questioned how I had even made it to this point. It's amazing what confidence in God can do—even if it's not His will. This job opportunity looked like God's leading because of the Wells Fargo wheel, but unfortunately this was not the wheel that was prophesied to me.

Proverbs 3:3-6

"Trust in the LORD with all your heart And do not lean on your own understanding. In all your ways acknowledge Him, And He will make your paths straight."

Chapter Four

Could this be the Wheel?

My mother called. "Cris, the wheel mobile is coming to Milwaukee! Promise me you'll go and try out!" Mom was a religious Wheel of Fortune watcher. Her friends knew not to call between 6:30 and 7 pm. She of all people would know where that wheel mobile would be. I hesitantly agreed because of my busy schedule without even acknowledging the fact that this could be God's wheel for my life. Anytime the phone rang and it was her, it was always a reminder call about the upcoming audition to ease her mind that I wouldn't forget. Finally the day came when I replied, "*Yes* mom, I am on my way down there right now." I love the way she loved me and wanted good things for me. She was the best example of Christ's love than anyone else in my life. I also believe that the power of her prayers is what brought about this wonderful opportunity.

The auditions were held in Milwaukee at Steinhafel's—a large furniture store that held the 10,000 people that showed up for the auditions. While inching my way forward in line to enter the building, I befriended a few other females who shared in my excitement of possibly being selected. We shared about our lives, dreamed together about winning, and stuck together through the audition process. We were given cards to fill out telling about ourselves, our talents, and why we would make good candidates for the show. On mine I wrote that I love to sing. It has always been a passion of mine. I also noted that I was writing a book (Stepping Higher—watch for it in the future.) I wasn't sure why they asked some of the questions they did, but I assumed it was relevant to what they were looking for in a contestant.

My new friends and I settled in our seats and were bracing ourselves to be called at any time. I was in my "element." I love to be around people and this was very exciting for me. They selected people for 3 different auditions from a spinning cage that held our information cards. Individuals were called up to the stage and were asked to introduce themselves and perform a talent listed on their cards. I enjoyed watching the people perform their talents and play the part in a mock game show. I wasn't selected that day and decided to meet up with the females the next day for the second and last day of the auditions.

The next day was just as exciting as the first. As the first and second auditions had passed, I did not think I would be called up. I brought it up to God, "I don't know why you have me here." Right in the middle of this conversation with the Lord, I heard my name being called out. "Never mind!" I immediately ended my conversation with God as I bolted toward the stage. My heart was pounding and I was so excited. I smiled for a camera and grabbed the forms they instructed me to fill out. I made sure to listen and follow any and all directions that were given.

Earlier I imagined that if I wrote singing as one of my talents that I would be asked to do so. I didn't want to just sing a song like everyone else did, and my voice was strained from shouting for the news cameras all day. "10 AT 10!" (meaning channel 10 at 10:00) became our monotonous call. The lesson I planned to teach was how to open the vocal chords in a way that an opera singer would sing. This way we could belt out a loud sound without harming our throats. As I earlier predicted, they wanted me to sing so I carried out my plan. Out of my mouth I thundered "10 AT 10" in my opera style voice that was so loud it had the man hosting the audition jump away from me startled. I didn't realize how loud I sang it. "I think you should warn people if you ever do that again!" suggested the host amusedly. The audience laughed and I was relieved and delighted to move on to the game show portion of the audition. In the mock game, I called one letter that wasn't there and I didn't get another stab at it. The audience was deprived of more of my theatrical flair.

I got an email within months inviting me to come to a second audition. It covered the logistics and instructions and included a warning of how difficult it is to be selected. At this point, I wasn't overly concerned if I didn't make it on the show. My life was being led by God and the outcomes were up to Him as well. This second audition was in a smaller venue that slashed the 10,000 participants down to 100.

The show crew gave instructions on what they were looking for. I noticed that many of the other candidates failed to be enthusiastic in hand motions, volume of their voice, and couldn't muster up the strength to spin an invisible thousand pound wheel. Later, on the news, they covered the timid as well as the boistrous. Needless to say, that camera was in my favor because they showed me hamming it up. I was described as "one who fared better." All I know is I was enjoying it thoroughly.

Once the second audition was over, we were told the final decision would come in the mail if we were selected to be a contestants, and it could be up to a year before they would contact you. In the mailing it would give the show date and instructions. As far as any expectations or anxiety of being on the show, I, again, had it in my mind to leave any and all results in God's hands. I had to return to work that Monday, and as far as I was concerned I still had financial hurdles to deal with and needed to plan some kind of action towards getting out of it.

I started to pursue filing for bankruptcy because of the daily accumulation of credit card fees, because it seemed to be my only alternative. I didn't feel it would be God's will for me to file for bankruptcy and I let Him know that. I was still hanging onto the fact that I was like an Israelite in the desert where God would provide my way out of the enslaving debt and into a financial freedom.

Jeremiah 29:11-14

"For I know the plans I have for you," declares the Lord, "plans to prosper you and not to harm you, plans to give you hope and a future. Then you will call on me and come and pray to me, and I will listen to you. You will seek me and find me when you seek me with all your heart. I will be found by you," declares the Lord, "and will bring you back from captivity."

Chapter Five

Chosen

We can go about our life as Christians thinking we are walking in the faith, yet sometimes we become dry as if in a parched desert place. It seems we have stopped taking the time to go into the intimate place of being in God's presence, and it shows in our attitudes. We can be on the mountaintop loving others one day, and the next be on the defense, completely tied up in all the cares of the world. I happened to be in this spiritually dry place during this time of transition. I woke up one morning in anguish and pain over my previous days behavior. "How can you want me to be yours and call me a Christian, Lord?" were all I could muster for my first words to God. "I cannot go out into the world today or I am afraid I will be hurting others again." I made a pact that I would stay safe under my covers where I wouldn't be hurting anyone. I thought I had been trusting God for my financial situation but it seems I had been letting worry take the best of me. But God would have nothing to do with my pre planned pity party. He immediately spoke to my spirit reminding me that He chose me.

1 Peter 2:9
"But you are a CHOSEN race, a royal priesthood, a holy nation, a people for God's God's own possession, so that you may proclaim the excellencies of Him who has called you out of darkness into His marvelous light;

Ephesians 1:4-5
"...just as He chose us in Him before the foundation of the world, that we would be holy and blameless before Him In love He predestined us to adoption as sons through Jesus Christ to Himself, according to the kind intention of His will..."

Years earlier while in AA, my sponsor would always tell me to "suit up and show up." It was advice that I have used on many days when I didn't want to face the world. The message she was relaying to me was to turn off my negative thoughts and the tangled emotions going on in my heart and as if I were a robot to get dressed and show up for life. She reminded me that every time I would do this, within no time, I would be seeing life differently than when I woke up. This seemed to be the same thing that God was putting on my heart this particular morning as well. He nudged me to get dressed and show up for life and not worry about hurting others, because I was not the one that was changing me but He was as long as I wanted Him to.

Ezekiel 36:26
"Moreover, I will give you a new heart and put a new spirit within you; and I will remove the heart of stone from your flesh and give you a heart of flesh."

I agreed to get up and face my day but reminded God that I could not be held responsible if I fell short again because I couldn't do it; I needed Him to do it in me. I don't want to excuse or disregard any of my own responsibility in my character but there are many times when we try to be good on our own abilities and we can't without God. It may seem that I was being a bit rebellious telling God that He would be the one held responsible but I believe that He is ok when we live with Him in a real way. He is my friend that I can trust and He understands my heart even when my moods seem to be contradicting it.

I applied my make up, ate a little breakfast, and got ready to head out the door with the attitude to apologize to everyone that I came in contact with that had to deal with my recent behavior.

On my drive to work, I made my usual stop at the post office. I used a P.O. box for my mail since I would just be at Theresa's temporarily. I didn't want to have to leave Theresa a mail trail that would continue to come to her house long after I had moved. I hurried in to get my mail and noticed there was an envelope from Wheel of Fortune. Once in my car I ripped it open immediately. Tears started to flow out of my eyes when I read the top of the letter.

"CONGRATULATIONS, YOU HAVE BEEN CHOSEN"

I knew in my spirit that this letter was not just referring to Wheel of Fortune but God was confirming His presence in my life and His hand of love. My heart was deeply touched and I cried. He touched me on a day I least deserved

35

it. Nothing compares to when God shows Himself in my life. Nothing.

I arrived to work with no make up on my face but a smile that stretched as far as my cheeks could go. On a morning that I didn't want to face the world, here I was shining God's light brighter than any star an astronomer would dare to compete with. His kindness is the most powerful way He uses to change us. He really is an awesome God.

Romans 15:13

May the God of hope fill you with all joy and peace as you trust in him, so that you may overflow with hope by the power of the Holy Spirit.

Chapter Six

Getting Ready for the Show

The letter from Wheel of Fortune gave all the needed instructions for me to plan and prepare. I had to ask off of work for my trip to California, which was the first and probably only time that an employer will be excited for me to take time away! The company I worked for were so supportive and fun to share this exciting time in my life with. I heard giggles from the sales people that passed by while I practiced with a DVD version of the game on my computer during my lunch breaks. Because of all the job losses I had experienced prior to this job, it was refreshing to be appreciated and a sense of job security there. If God hadn't eventually moved me on I would still be there today.

After informing my job, I then made the traveling arrangements for myself and my oldest son, Paul, who was excited to come and support me. My brother, Tony arranged to come and meet us there from Colorado. I felt blessed to have them to share this with me. Because of my mother's health she was not able to fly out and support me there, but I felt very supported in her prayers for me from home. I had also hoped my youngest son Mathew could be there to share this with me as well, but he was needed at his job in Pennsylvania, but he, too, kept me covered in prayer.

While packing I made sure to follow each instruction given with the letter. The instructions included to bring 3 outfits just in case something spilled or they wanted me to change clothes for any reason. The outfits they preferred were to be in solid colors that worked best for the appearance with camera viewing. As I proceeded to pull everything out of my closet to choose these outfits, the word ketchup came to my mind. "Wow" I thought. "Ketchup would make a great bonus round word. No one would want to call a K, C, H, P or U! They'll have to use *that* word someday!"

If you have never watched the game show or don't understand how the bonus round works, it consists of calling out letters to guess a word or phrase. The game show supplies the most frequently used letters in words: R,S,T,L,N and E. The contestant then has to choose 4 consonants and 1 vowel to guess the phrase. In my practicing, I had planned to use the letters M, D, F and A if I were to make it to the bonus round.

I couldn't bring my entire closet so I chose my clothes carefully, and still the word ketchup invaded my mind. It seemed to not go away. I made a comment to God once I realized it was Him, "Alright already, I get it God... KETCHUP!"

I exclaimed, in a humorous but confused tone. Without a doubt in my mind, I knew this nudging was of Him. I didn't know what ketchup had to do with anything, but because of my relationship with Him I've come to know His voice.

One of my favorite passages in the Bible about God's voice is in John 10:27 that tells about Jesus as a shepherd, and His flock of sheep that know Him. A shepherd is one that adores His sheep, protects them from harm, feeds them, and disciplines them so they go in the right direction. With all of this care and attention, the sheep know the shepherd's voice. The sheep are in a direct relationship with the shepherd. My sons, with whom I share close relationships, have voices that I could distinguish above any other. If my son Paul were calling out to me from another room saying, "Hey Mom!" I would know immediately that it was him, even though I couldn't see him. I know my son's voice. This is how God desires us to know Him as well. We can only truly know His voice when we know Him.

Paul arrived early the next morning—right on time. A perfect gentleman I might add. He grabbed my suitcases and placed them in his trunk. He then opened the door for me. This is something he does often, and I always feel so blessed by it. Paul is a very deep and compassionate man who has a way of doing special things for people. It is so touching especially for me, his mom. I can't help but to brag about it!

Psalm 127:3
"Behold, children are a heritage from the Lord, the fruit of the womb a reward."

Once settled in the car and on our way to the airport, I updated Paul on my previous night's experience, "The Lord will not leave me alone with the word Ketchup!" I exclaimed. Paul agreed thinking, "Yeah God, she needs to catch up on her bills." With God, there can be a double meaning of words and this was definitely an example of that. Paul had heard "catch up" where I had heard "ketchup."

When we arrived in California, we met up with Tony at the hotel. We then spent the day sightseeing around Hollywood and enjoying the warm sun. Paul and I had just left Wisconsin's chilly wind—a welcoming difference. The next day, I had to be at Universal Studios bright and early in the morning. It was the big day of the show. Our hotel was walking distance away. Paul and Tony would be walking over later, because they were a part of the audience. Once I was there, I had to wait for all the other contestants to arrive, and then we were then led through the back of the huge building. Walking through, I felt like an ant. All I could do was imagine that God's storehouse would be even bigger than this. The storage area was so large that even Jeeps sat on shelves with many other large movie props.

The Wheel of Fortune area we were led to, had a room I like to refer to as the "party room." This is where we were given instructions in an energetic atmosphere to pump us up for the show. As contestants we picked numbered balls to see what show we would be on. My ball had the number 5, which meant my show would be Friday's show. Each ball represented the day of the week with Monday as ball 1 and Tuesday, ball 2 and so on. I've always referred to the number 5 as a spiritual number that symbolizes grace, so by picking that number I was really feeling that grace. I then found the other contestants for Friday's show, and we introduced ourselves to each other. We were led to the room with the actual thousand pound wheel. We were then given more details on what to do, where to look, etcetera for the taping of the show.

I was the last person to go into the make up room but was not the least. It just so happened that Vanna needed to have her make up refreshed after me. She was wearing a bright orange T Shirt but her smile was even brighter. Sometimes when encountering celebrities you might expect them to be somewhat arrogant, but she carried a warmth in her countenance that to me was very pleasant.

The people were all so wonderful and fun. During the excitement and wardrobe approval, I learned that many females are sent home because they don't have the right apparel. They maybe didn't read the instructions that came with the letter specifically stating that it was a family game show, which requires non-revealing blouses. I also learned that the people in California cannot be scheduled contestants, but are able to be extras for situations like this. The state restricts their residents from becoming professional game show contestants.

Once I had my wardrobe approved and make up perfected, I sat and sipped on some coffee amused at my surroundings. Through the voices and laughing, I heard my name being called out in the distance. I immediately got up to see who it was. I noticed a man peering through a door and went to see what he wanted. I thought maybe he needed to look over my outfit or prepare me more for the show. "Follow me," he said in a low voice, and he led me to his desk. He held up some forms I filled out earlier and inquired about my past felony. I said reassuringly, "It's true, but I also gave this information on all the audition forms, and it hasn't been a problem up until now." He chuckled, "Don't worry about it! I just needed to know what the conviction was for." He informed me that I only told about my new changed life with Jesus and not the reason for the arrest. I let out a sigh of relief and explained that I sold cocaine to an undercover officer years ago. "That is all I needed to know," he expressed, "have a great game!"

There is a sense of peace when we know that we are forgiven by God of our past. We can trust that anything we have done or do is not being held against us by God. God's main desire is for us to see our need for Him and allow his transformation to change us while finding ourselves fall even deeper in love with Him.

One last exciting thing to mention is that when Wheel of Fortune tapes their shows, they tape all the days of the week in one day. Since my show was day 5 my show would be aired on a Friday, therefore I had to wait until the other four days were taped. Can you imagine being a game show host and only working one day a week?

While waiting for my show's time I watched the other tapings from upstairs—adjacent to the audience. It was forbidden to have any eye contact with the audience, especially with the people who came to support you. I dared not look at Paul and Tony at any time while there even though it would have been great to see where they were sitting.

As I watched their games I started to feel a little light headed and jittery and realized that I was not doing well in guessing any of the puzzles for the shows before mine. I panicked because I couldn't concentrate. I prayed, "Lord, what I am I going to do? I am not getting any of these puzzles, I should have never had that cup of coffee earlier!" I'm not like other people; coffee does the opposite for me. Rather than giving me energy, I felt even less alert. Brain dead would be a good way to explain it. I happened to look up while my inquiry with God and saw the game's "Theme of the Week" board before my eyes. It was a beautiful image of warm sands, cactus plants, and a blazing sun. The words describing this theme of the week silenced me from my complaining to God as it read, "Desert Passage." I don't think God could have spoken any clearer than at that moment. His presence was there and He was going to lead me out of my desert place and into a new promised land—just like He promised the

Israelites. I didn't have to worry about performing or failing in any way because God already had everything covered. He was in control, and all I needed to do was to have peace, to trust Him, and to enjoy this wonderful and exhilarating opportunity.

Isaiah 58:11

"And the LORD will continually guide you, And satisfy your desire in scorched places, And give strength to your bones; And you will be like a watered garden, And like a spring of water whose waters do not fail.

Chapter Seven

Desert Passage

It was finally time for my show. I quickly made my way down to the taping stage to meet with the other contestants. They rigged up microphones on us and gave a recap of how to play, where to look for our scores, and each round's information. We each had a chance to practice giving the wheel a spin. Here it was—time to start taping the show. Pat Sajak, the host, asked each of us to share about ourselves to which he was ready with humorous comebacks. I was nervous, but I kept a smile and played the part as best as I could. Normally I don't have a problem talking, but here I was fumbling with my words. I really wasn't myself at all, not only because of my nerves, but being under the influence of the caffeinated coffee. It definitely is much harder to be there in person in front of the cameras and play well than in the comfort of your own home. At home, in your own comfy chair, you're not worrying about a world of people watching you and having to remember where to look for the letters called and scores. The Lord says that He is strong in our weaknesses (2 Corinthians 12:10), and that is what I believe was happening for me most of that day. I was in His strength and not my own and feeling very grateful.

I made it through the short introductions and now it was time to move on to the game. The best way to describe Wheel Of Fortune is that it is a word game similar to hangman. The objective is to guess the missing letters until you recognize the complete word or phrase. The game has categories of words and phrases for example; things, people, places, food, and so on.

If you've never seen the show, there are prizes on the wheel as well as prize puzzles. Prize puzzles are somewhat described by the puzzle and prizes on the wheel are attainable by landing on them. If you guess the right phrase or word you get to keep the prize. The wheel can also land on unpleasant areas such as bankruptcy, which is losing the total amount accumulated for that round or prize puzzle. There is also a "lose a turn" on the wheel, and the person loses their turn but also keeps what they accumulated for that round with hopes to get another chance to solve the puzzle.

During the first round, I landed on the $10,000 space that is nestled between two bankrupts. I picked up the card and showed it off. It is a very hard and rare place for the wheel to land because of how small it was crammed between the two bankruptcies. The category to this first round was titled "THING." I bought vowels whenever I could to help give me time to look over the puzzle. It seemed to go so fast. It was hard to observe the puzzle when spinning the wheel! It helped that Pat would keep telling me how much money I had or what my next options were. Vowels could be purchased for $250 even if there were more than one in the puzzle. Buying the vowels also helped me get a feel of what other letters might be in the word and I somehow kept guessing the correct letters (God in me?) and was able to stay in the round. As it was getting close to the point where there was only a couple of letters left, I still was clueless to what the word was. I realized that the second word was coastline. "What kind of coastline is a thing?" I thought. I spun again. This time everyone was on the edge of their seat because there were only 2 letters left. Was I the only one who didn't know it? Finally I ended up with one letter left in the first word and coastline in the second word of this thing. It appeared as "_RAMATIC COASTLINE." I needed that one letter before the R and it appeared it could be dramatic. I don't know about you but I never heard of a beach referred to as a "dramatic coastline" and I wouldn't have considered it a thing over a place at the time, but it was all I could think of so I took a stab at it and guessed "dramatic coastline". The music started to play and everyone was clapping. I won that round. It happened to be a prize puzzle that included a trip to Bermuda (that must where I would experience the dramatic coastline.) My total for that round was $17,800! I hugged Pat and thanked him while subconsciously thanking God.

The other two contestants started to catch up to me, but I am grateful to say that they never made it. Because of my high total of $17,800 from that one round I was the final winner. I then went to the Bonus Round to have a chance to win bigger money or prizes. The wonderful thing about this game show is that the other two contestants were also winners. They didn't lose any of the money they won during the other rounds of the game. I was able to see them after the show, and they both were happy for me and grateful for their own winnings. Another great thing about the show is that if you are not fortunate enough to win any rounds you will still be awarded a $1,000 parting gift--almost like the flashlight when parting with my job after the conference. The $1,000 they send people off with helps the contestant cover the flight and and other expenses.

Pat led me down to a smaller wheel that held envelopes that contained bigger prizes. I was told to spin it so Pat could pick the envelope it landed on before we headed over to the last and final puzzle. The category for this puzzle was "Food and Drink." As I looked up and heard the noises for each of the popular letters being revealed, it was as if I were being taken up into another realm of heaven standing upon the shiniest floor I have ever been on. The letters that were being revealed in this one word food and drink category were E and T. In bold letters it appeared: _ E T _ _ _ _. I knew it was ketchup because of the Lord so graciously telling me this word when I was packing. This was all so surreal. I was standing in the presence of the Lord and in a place of feeling unworthy of such an act of kindness from the living God and what He was doing for me.

I found it somewhat difficult to call out K,C,P, and U to finish the game without releasing the held back ocean of tears that wanted to burst forth from my eyes. I made it through, barely. Pat seemed to notice my countenance and saved the day by jokingly stating, "You must think you're pretty smart!" I laughed as well as the audience. Then before my eyes, the letters I just guessed appeared. It *really* was the word ketchup! Even though I know God talks to me, here I was experiencing it more powerful than I could ever have imagined. I would have to set aside my deep emotions and that spiritual place of awe that I was in and continue to stay on earth as a contestant on this game show even though I couldn't disregard how close God was.

With everything going on I forgot that there was still a prize. Thinking we had gone to commercial, I excitedly shared with Pat "I told Paul the Lord was giving me the word ketchup!" While I was sharing this with Pat he began to open the envelope that would reveal my prize. One thing that I noticed about Pat's talent in being a game show host is how attentive he is to what people say. He has a gift to find a witty comeback to just about anything anyone says, and he had one for me here as well. His reply to God giving me the word was, "WELL HE IS ALSO GIVING YOU $30,000!" My grand total ended up being $47,800!

God was also doing incredible things in other people. My son, Paul, told me after the show that just before he and my brother, Tony, came up to the stage and share in the excitement, the director was frantic; he heard me tell Pat that I was given the answer. I can easily understand why he was upset; because of all the precautions that they take to make sure that no one cheats. "What should we do? What should we do?" he anxiously inquired but the man who spoke with me about my conviction and my changed life with Jesus, grabbed the director by the shoulders to calm him down. He said "Don't worry about it, God is the one that gave her the answer." I know God touched my life by His presence, and I have a feeling that He was weaving revelation of His presence in others lives as well.

Later when I took my puzzle prize trip to Bermuda, God led me in a situation to be on their TV station. I was interviewed about my Wheel of Fortune experience and it aired three nights in a row. I wanted to see the DVD since I didn't get to watch it while vacationing. On the plane when I placed it in my computer, it was blank. There was nothing on it. I was disappointed about it, but God seemed to speak to my spirit telling me that the outcome of that show was not my business to know. There could have been many people watching that gave their hearts to God, but whatever was going on was God's business. I gave Him my life to use me and to leave the outcome up to Him. It seemed as though He was picking me up and placing me where He wanted me.

I will never see ketchup the same again. One night out for dinner with my son, Paul, he amusingly squeezed ketchup all over his food to celebrate my victory. As I watched the ketchup flow from the bottle I thought of how it represented Christ's blood to me. It was the blood that paid my debt. We may never fully understand why Christ had to die on the cross, but because of a spiritual battle with God's enemy, there had to be a blood sacrifice. All throughout the Old Testament, the people of God sacrificed the blood of animals to atone for their sins and keep them in a right standing with God. There were many laws that no one could be perfect enough to fulfill. God will someday restore all things to be the way that He originally created them to be, without evil, and part of that plan is by sending Jesus to give up His blood on the cross. His blood is the final atonement for us to be right with God. If we invite Jesus in our life to be our Lord, he then makes a promise to us: He has a place for us in heaven and will also be in us on earth.

As far as my winnings, I didn't get to take home the money right away. They send out a check that could take up to 18 months to arrive and mine came just before then. The money would be just about enough to pay my debt. I was able to take care of myself with the new job, and I also settled into a new apartment. Even though I didn't have the money yet, it was a relief knowing it was coming. Once taxes and debt was paid off, the monetary total came to almost exactly what I needed and not much more. God was giving me what I needed but not making me rich. It was the same for the Israelites in the desert. They, too, were given just what they needed. He sent down like dew, a daily portion of bread called manna to eat. Nothing more and nothing less. He fed them and took care of them and was always with them. This "bread" God was providing for me was in the form of money, but it was just what I needed, nothing more and nothing less.

New Doors

Here I was with a new job, new apartment, and new hope. Just as John Chacha preached, it seemed that God was doing new things in my life and opening new doors. I started doing an online ministry school with Morningstar. This then led me to move there a year later to complete my second year degree. I was able to share this wonderful testimony to many people and was interviewed with their online show. I started getting dozens of emails from people all over the world telling me how this testimony changed their lives, even to the point of financial miracles in their own lives. One couple said it was within minutes of hearing my story that debtors released their debt. Revelation 12:11 in the Bible states, *"They triumphed over him (Satan) by the blood of the Lamb and by the word of their testimony; that there is power in the testimony"*. These responses proved that to me in a very special way.

Life with God is a journey, and I am finding more each day that it is never boring. It may be extremely challenging like a roller coaster ride—ups and downs. Through all the transitions, He is constant and I can always expect to be transformed closer to His perfect likeness. I may be far from what He is transforming me to become, but I thank God that He has not kept me who I used to be.

2 Corinthians 5:17

Therefore, if anyone is in Christ, the new creation has come: The old has gone, the new is here!

Chapter Eight

Supernatural Touches

Heading home from Hollywood, in the plane from my amazing experience, I snuggled on my pillow and decided to nap. As I woke up, I saw the most beautiful view. This view was not out the airplane window but instead was in the seat beside me. It was of my son Paul. He had his tray set down, his bible open and was writing in his songbook. Paul enjoys writing songs and creating music. At the time his interest was in hip-hop, and unfortunately most of the songs were not about God. Years earlier, he started to drift from the Lord and his music reflected that. Here in front of my eyes was Paul writing a song with an open Bible. God was finding His way back into Paul's heart. I quickly closed my eyes and rested my head back on my pillow. I didn't want to interrupt what

God was doing there. My heart again was deeply touched by God's kindness because of all the worrying and praying I had done for my son. I suppose it was like what my mother had done for me and my finances; God was showing off. He continued to show his presence even after the miracle wheel.

One example of God showing His help was with a tiny precious butterfly. It may not sound too supernatural for God to use a butterfly because they are so common, but I've had other experiences with butterflies to know that this one was also from God. On this particular day and that tiny butterfly, Paul and I were on our way of moving me to the Carolinas to start my second year with Morningstar's ministry school. I had a loaded up Ryder truck with all my belongings. About half the way on our 15-hour drive, the truck started to putter out. Paul began to become a little distressed asking what we should do once pulled over and stopped. The butterfly flew onto the windshield as if to say, "hello, I am here" and then flew off into the distance. I reassured Paul that God was with us because of that butterfly. Immediately Paul's countenance changed to one of wonder. "Really mom, you think so?" I called the truck company and they sent someone out to pick us up. They towed the truck in and moved all my things to a new truck. They gave us snacks to eat and I was told that they were drastically reducing my cost for the truck. This was a needed help because even though I won on the game show, there was not much left after paying off my debts. Here God was blessing me financially again in order to move me out to the ministry.

If God has a plan and a will for our lives, He will take care of everything that is needed for this to take place. He also had a will and a plan for my life to know Him not as just a friend but also as a father. I can't believe I am actually writing those words, "God the father." To me whenever I would hear this expression of God, as being a father figure, it seemed to be a religious connotation but not something personal. I couldn't view God as a father because of my experience with my own father. It was not a loving or trusting relationship. I had a lot of anger towards him. Even though God has helped me to come to a place of forgiveness towards my father I still could not relate to God in that way. In the south they like to refer to God the father as "Papa". This was very foreign to me and I couldn't relate. It even made me uncomfortable.

My perspective about God as my father was changed through a message that Steve Thompson shared one Sunday morning at Morningstar. Steve shared about how he, as a father loved to bless his children. He then gave an example of taking his kids to an amusement park. He would pull out his wallet and totally be in the "great dad" mode. If one of his children wanted cotton candy out came a few bills from his wallet. What? Another wanted to go on a ride? "Ok, here is a couple more dollars." Steve was blessed, as he was able to bless and give good things to his children. He also shared in this message how it would not be the same if someone else's kids came for a handout too. His kids are special to him. Steve went on to share that he believed God wanted me to know that the Lord blessed me through Wheel of Fortune to help me to understand Him as my father that loved and cared for me and wanted to bless me with good things. God wanted me to know that I was His daughter. I am one of the living God's children and am no longer fatherless. I am glad to say that I would no longer be uncomfortable to call him Papa.

Steve also shared how a woman approached him regarding my testimony and winning on the game show. This woman seemed to say that God would not allow one person to win and the others to lose, because it would not be fair. Steve then held up his Bible and asked the congregation to show him in it where God was fair. No one came up to the challenge. God is a good God but carries out His purposes the way He desires. He gives us good things at times, and other times, it may not be so easy, but we can trust that He loves us, has compassion for us and His intensions are for our good for us to know His goodness.

Psalm 8:4

"....what is mankind that you are mindful of them, human beings that you care for them?'

Chapter Nine

God Can Do It Again

After several years at Morningstar I found myself in a place of financial hardship again. The circumstances were different because this time it involved my health. God allows the trials in our lives to strengthen us but I felt like all the life was sucked out of me. I was once again broke and had no home to call my own. I had a hard time worshipping and praising God like I did before. I was no longer able to pay rent or buy food and I needed to figure out what to do. Again, I felt like an Israelite wandering the desert looking for a home. I even felt some anger toward God for having me to face this again. "How in the world could God help me again?" I thought. I packed up what I could fit in my car and drove back to Wisconsin. I wasn't running from anything or going to anything. I just needed to move on because it seemed God was not allowing me to stay there. I was financially drained and no job options were available. If anyone knows how to get a job, it's me. I have experienced this many times but it seemed to me that God was nudging me to go back to Wisconsin where my family was and I decided to be obedient.

I was offered a room with a very generous woman, Mary, and found a job quickly. My health was better because I had some time to heal from a surgery. Even though I obtained a job, it took several weeks before I had any income. One night I couldn't sleep and I decided to look up ways for possible quick income opportunities that might be available in my area. I came across an ad to be on a game show. It was called "Let's Ask America. "I applied, not thinking any thing would come of it, but I filled it out anyway. Within the week someone had called me and wanted to Skype (video chat) with me regarding the game show I applied for. I was then interviewed by someone else a couple of days later through Skype again, who then scheduled me for a "mock" game show to see how I would do. They supplied me with cards to use on the show by sending them in the mail after I was accepted and the date was set.

The day came for the show and I happened to be in a very bad place emotionally because of my financial situation. I was placing my worth on my financial security. I felt weak and couldn't even laugh. I couldn't seem to concentrate to answer the questions because my mind was in a fog of self doubt. Depression oozed through my pores. Everyone from the show was surprised at my change of personality but because they believed in me. They agreed to schedule me for a different day.

God's grace is amazing. He wouldn't leave me alone with a song like He didn't leave me alone with the word

Ketchup. The song was by Bill Withers called "Ain't No Sunshine." The Lord seemed to be telling me that if He resides in me if I am no longer sharing myself with Him that He wanted me back.

"Ain't no sonshine when she's gone
Only darkness every day.
Ain't no sonshine when she's gone
And this house just ain't no home
Anytime she goes away."

The Lord was nudging and wooing me back and because of my love for Him I decided to hang in there. The day of the show, I was in a better place. I made the decision to again trust God and to praise Him. It is amazing the peace and joy that comes from praising the Lord and keeping Him close. My worth is not in my circumstances but in God. *Let's Ask America* is a game show that consists of 4 people who play from their homes, or chosen places to be viewed from, that are video Skyped into the Hollywood studio to participate as contestants. It also consists of a live audience; a host and questions that pertain to what different people in America would answer to certain situations. The object is to guess the correct answer. This game show is like Wheel of Fortune in the way that it ends with one winner to go for the round, but this game show does it through a process of elimination.

The key to doing well is paying attention to who is being asked. For example men in their 30's could be for one question and middle aged woman for another. One of the questions I was asked was "What would new dads in their 30's say was the hardest thing to adjust to after the baby was born?" While giving our answers we were also told to be ready to give our reasons for our selections. The answers to select for this question that I was to pick from were;

1. Changing Diapers
2. Getting Up At All Hours
3. Baby Stuff Everywhere
4. Their wife's mood swings

I chose "Getting up at all hours" for my answer because it seemed to me to be the hardest part for men who have been working for years to adjust to. Keeping in mind that the survey was for new dads in their 30's but if it were new dads in their 20's I might have not selected that answer. I won $10,000 just sitting in front of my computer in my son's living room. I can no longer doubt and say God will not do it again, because He did.

As you read my testimony you may think that your "case" is different. You may think that good things won't happen for you like they did for me. Maybe you have a terminal illness or a handicap that is preventing you from being blessed the way you would like to be blessed. Even though your circumstances may be different, your solution can be the same. God is the solution to all of our trails in life. Many times it is a privilege to have these trials because of how we are strengthened in them if we go through them with God. By staying focused on the Holy Spirit in our life we will begin to see Him more often and experience Him in many surprising ways. Just like the Israelites in the desert, God was with them and had a plan.

Romans 5:3 says "...but we also glory in our sufferings, because we know that suffering produces perseverance; perseverance, character; and character, hope."

If there is power in a testimony then I pray that you as the reader are not only empowered for miracles but to also overcome anything that is keeping you from what God has for you in your life, especially hearing Him speak to you.

By praising Him and trusting Him you will go through everything you face with more peace and will find yourself amazed at what He will do for you.

I also want to add that if we ever think that God would not use a secular game show or secular song then we are putting Him in a religious box. God can use anything. Everything is under Him.

2 Corinthians 1:10

"He has delivered us from such a deadly peril, and he will deliver us again. On him we have set our hope that he will continue to deliver us..."

Isaiah 40:31

"But they that wait upon the LORD shall renew their strength; they shall mount up with wings as eagles; they shall run, and not be weary; and they shall walk, and not faint."

James 1:2-3

Dear brothers and sisters, when troubles of any kind come your way, consider it an opportunity for great joy. For you know that when your faith is tested, your endurance has a chance to grow.

The End

About the Author

Cristi Winkler is a graduate with an associate's degree with Morningstar Ministries (MSU). She holds a certificate in Christian counseling and has served in ministry in many different ways, including teaching and training in the prophetic, facilitating house groups/bible studies, etc. She is also licensed in Cosmetology.

Ms. Winkler is currently writing articles for an online ministry magazine GlobalPropheticvoice.com out of Chicago IL. She has interviewed and written articles on missionaries for Morningstar Ministries Mission Department (CMM). She also enjoys writing songs and even sang one of her tunes on a national game show "Let's Ask America". She has appeared on two televised game shows and is known by others to have a "Game Show Anointing" because of how God has used this avenue to bless her financially.

Cristi is also a mother of two grown sons and considers herself a young grandmother of two precious granddaughters. She is also a spiritual mother to other young woman. The most important relationship in her life is her relationship with Jesus.

Ms. Winkler is also a public speaker whose life aim and motivation is to give encouragement and hope to others as well as direction from wisdom she has gained through not only her own personal experiences but also through research and studies and most importantly through the Holy Spirit.

Made in the USA
San Bernardino, CA
06 August 2016